THE VISITOR

C000018537

Orkney

Lindsey Porter

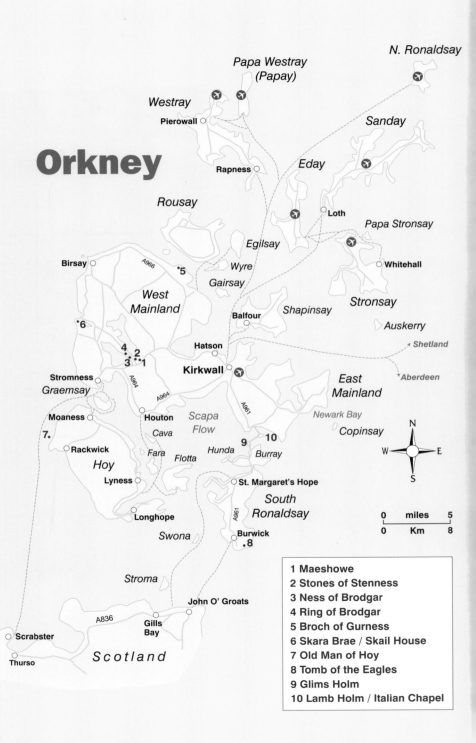

Orkney

N. Ronaldsay

Papa Westray
(Papay)

Westray

Pierowall

Sanday

Rapness

Eday

Rousay

Loth

Papa Stronsay

Egilsay

Birsay

A966

•5

Wyre

Whitehall

Gairsay

West
Mainland

•6

Stronsay

Balfour

Shapinsay

Auskerry

Hatson

4 2
3 1

Kirkwall

Shetland

Aberdeen

Stromness

East
Mainland

Graemsay

A964

A964

A961

Moaness

Houton

Scapa
Flow

Newark Bay

Copinsay

7.

Cava

Rackwick

Fara

Flotta

Hunda

9

10

Burray

N

Hoy

Lyness

St. Margaret's Hope

W   E

Longhope

A961

South
Ronaldsay

S

Swona

Burwick

•8

0   miles   5

0   Km   8

Stroma

John O' Groats

Scrabster

A836

Gills
Bay

Thurso

Scotland

1 Maeshowe
2 Stones of Stenness
3 Ness of Brodgar
4 Ring of Brodgar
5 Broch of Gurness
6 Skara Brae / Skail House
7 Old Man of Hoy
8 Tomb of the Eagles
9 Glims Holm
10 Lamb Holm / Italian Chapel

Ring of Bodgar

Contents

Above: Pottery in former water mill, Shapinsay

Top Tips

Kirkwall
Explore the capital: Viking Cathedral, Earl's Palace ruins, and lots of local products for sale in narrow main street.

Stromness
The second town; historic shipping port with unusually narrow main street with narrow passages to properties.

Maeshowe/Ring of Brodgar Area
World Heritage site for prehistoric remains on several sites. Very impressive, especially Maeshowe, 1,500 years older than Stonehenge.

Kirkwall
Distillery Tours
Kirkwall has two distilleries, Scarpa and Highland Park, the most northerly malt whisky distillery in the world.

Newark Bay
If you fancy a deserted, sandy bay and its not too windy, try Newark Bay (p.23)

Outer Islands
Take a trip to one of the northern islands; Rousay for a close one and out to Westray or North Ronaldsay for a longer journey plus those in between. All have a special quality found only on small islands.

Hoy
Take the ferry from Stromness or Houton. Visit the beach at Rackwick, the old Man of Hoy (two hour walk) and Longhope in the south.

Tours
Check out the organised tours to Hoy and elsewhere and let someone else do the organising!

Italian Chapel, Lamb Holm
Built by Italian prisoners-of-war (see photo, p. 26). Explore South Ronaldsay beyond

Tomb of The Eagles, South Ronaldsay
Visitor Centre and trip into chambered tomb where 16,000 human and animal bones were found. Good interpretive centre with craft shop and café.

Craft Trail
Follow the brown signs and visit some interesting craft centres in the islands.

Orkney

North of the Scottish mainland there are three groups of islands within the United Kingdom: Orkney, Shetland and tiny North Rona with a group of even smaller islands and reefs. Nearest to the mainland is Orkney, with the tip of South Ronaldsay only six miles/9km off the coast.

Orkney consists of 67 islands of which 21 are inhabited (68 in 1901), supporting a population of 20,000 (28,699 in 1901) with 7,600 in Kirkwall and 2,100 in Stromness. The islands are mainly low in height and benefit from the effect of The Gulf Stream. An exception is the northern half of Hoy which offers some good moorland walking both on high hills and through undulating countryside with one striking east – west valley across the width of the island at Rackwick. As with many of the Scottish Islands they exhibit wonderful scenery, an abundance of prehistoric remains, many in good order and memorable beaches composed of white sand. In the south-

Opposite: St Margaret's Hope, South
Ronaldsay
Below left: Kirkwall's Pipe Band
outside the Cathedral
Below: Shapinsay Harbour

west are significant cliffs, especially on Hoy. The islands extend to some 375sq miles (971sq km).

The main islands are included here commencing with Orkney Mainland, then the islands to the south and finally those to the north.

The shortest surface route to Orkney is Gills Bay (near John O' Groats) to St Margaret's Hope on South Ronaldsay. It has a land link (using causeways) with the Orkney mainland. Pulling out of Gills Bay, the large catamaran heads out to sea with the island of Stroma ahead. Its grassed surface is covered with the ruins of former crofts. Sailing up Scarpa Flow, you pass the remains of batteries built and used during two world wars, protecting the Flow from aerial attack. This is, however, recent history. Orkney has the remains of people who lived here 5,500 or so years ago. The reminders of their life on Orkney are substantial. Several are superb examples of building activity in a pre-iron era. They are truly remarkable.

Against this enduring heritage, the ferry passes the island of Flotta with its tower burning off waste gasses both day and night. There is still time to reflect what Stone Age man would have thought of that before the ship turns to starboard and heads around a headland for St Margaret's Hope. Ahead is a series of special islands with an incredible history of occupation by a series of different peoples. Its wildlife and scenery are special too. Welcome to the Norse islands which have kept some of that Viking culture in its everyday life; Orcadian life which begins just a few miles off the Scottish mainland. Welcome to Orkney, where the people are welcoming, its history and heritage fascinating and where memories linger of breathtaking landscapes, white beaches and the inner glow of Highland Park or Scarpa malt.

Stroma

This small Pentland Forth island is 3miles/6km long, 1m/2km wide and rises to a height of 174ft/53m at Cairn Hill. In 1901, 375 people lived here and it had a post office. However, it has been uninhabited since 1962 except for the lighthouse keeper who left in 1996 when the light was automated. Today it is still grazed by sheep taken across from the mainland, with ownership rested in the Highland Council Local Authority. There are over 50, mostly derelict, croft houses scattered across the island.

One property remains in use: it is the former Manse and is used by the farmer when tending the resident sheep, eg during lambing. Near the harbour is a mausoleum of the Kennedys, who owned the island in the 17th century.

There is a tidal race at either end of the island. At the north end, the race may develop into a whirlpool known locally as the Swilkie (after Swilkie Point). The race may affect the direction of shipping and you may notice the ferry avoiding it. The island is now a conservation area because of its wildlife, especially its bird population and rare plants.

North Coast Marine Adventures offer a RIB (Rigid inflatable boat) trip to Stroma. The boat takes up to 12 passengers, between Easter and early October, from John O'Groats.

Getting There

North Coast Marine Adventures
Longfield, Dunnet, By Thurso, Caithness
KW14 8YD
☎ 01955 611797
E: ncexplorer@northeast.fsnet.co.uk
Or contact Gills Bay piermaster

Accommodation

For Caithness (Mainland) accommodation contact:

The Tourist Information Booking Bureau
☎ 0131 625 8585
E: info@visitscotland.com
Or write to:

Visit Scotland
Ocean Point One
94 Ocean Drive
Edinburgh EH6 6JH

Swona Island

North of Stroma is Swona Island, which was inhabited until 1974. Some cattle were left on the island at that time and are now wild, recognised as a breed of their own. Swona is 1.25miles by 0.5 mile in extent, rising to 128ft (39m) in height. The island is now a Conservation Area.

Orkney Mainland

Approaching Mainland Orkney (St Margarets Hope) from Gills Bay (near John O' Groats) is probably the finest way of reaching Orkney. It is only a short distance (about 45 minutes across the Pentland Forth and into Scarpa Flow, but it is full of interest, passing islands now bereft of any community; the legacy of past defences; and the modern embrace of technology on Flotta, where the undersea pipeline bring its oil to our shores.

Kirkwall

This Viking city dates back from c. 1035 when a community was established by Earl Rognuald Brusason. The local Tourist Board claims that the 'original town is one of the best preserved examples of an ancient Norse Town'. Its vibrant community abuts its busy harbour, which now incorporates a 95 berth marina. In the heart of the city, in West Castle Street is The Tourist Information Centre, located near the Bus Station and incorporating the Travel Centre, where you can book accommodation or seek advice on your travel plans.

Many of the attractions here have links with the city's past:

The Cathedral, dedicated to the Viking St Magnus was founded in 1137 and repays a visit. There is also an upper floor tour if you can stand the heights. The interior of the church appears 'heavy' with large columns supporting the roof. There is, however, much of interest.

Originally part of the arch-diocese of Trondheim in Norway, it was ceded to the King of Scotland when both Shetland and Orkney were offered as surety for a dowry when the King married the daughter of the King of Denmark in 1468. Norway at that time was part of the Kingdom of Denmark. In 1486, the King of Scotland gave the cathedral to the people of Kirkwall and it is today still the property of the people of Orkney.

It is associated with St Magnus. He was joint Earl of Orkney with his cousin, who betrayed him and had him killed by an axe-blow to his head. His remains and those of his nephew Earl Rognvald (now St Rognvald) were found in separate columns in the cathedral in 1919 and re-interred in 1923. The east window is from the 13th century and the west window dates from late 14th-early 15th century. The aisle walls are covered with 17th century grave markers.

Outside the Cathedral in Broad Street, is the Mercat Cross of 1621 (the original is in the Cathedral against the east wall in the north transept and you are looking at a copy of it). At 1pm on Christmas Day and New Years Day, the annual Ba' Game is held. It is traditional hug football, played by Uppies and Doonies (up-street and down-street sides) through the streets of Kirkwall. There are at least 50 players on each side and the onlookers follow the play through the streets. The pattern of play, even some of the terminology used, is replicated at the Shrovetide games at Ashbourne in Derbyshire, England. There are other places on the Scottish mainland where an annual (Shrovetide) hug football game is still observed.

There is a Bishop's Palace nearby, originally built in the mid-12th century; it was rebuilt in the 15th century. The nearby Earl's Palace is not much later having been built in 1600 by Earl Patrick Stewart, with French Renaissance style architecture. There is a joint ticket for the Bishop's and Earl's Palaces, both of which are ruins. The Orkney Museum and gardens at Tankerness House is in one of the city's finest town houses and covers the rich archaeological heritage of Orkney.

Coming out of the Cathedral, the Bishops and Earls Palaces are off the street to the left side. At the bottom is one of Kirkwall's bookshops and to

Above left: Stroma & mausoleum

Above right: oats drying in stooks at Kirkwall

Left: Swona Island, now deserted

Below left: Kirkwall Cathedral

Below right: The Earl's Palace

Left: Kirkwall Harbour **Right:** Albert Street, Kirkwall

the right is Albert Street, the principal shopping street. If you walk to the end and turn left, you are walking straight towards the harbour.

As a contrast, you can visit the Highland Park Distillery. It was established in 1798 and tours are available. It is rated a 5-star visitor attraction and of course incorporates a shop for the inevitable purchase. It is the most northerly malt whisky distillery in the world, with the more recently re-established Scarpa distillery half a mile short of the record.

There is also a Health Centre and Swimming Pool housed at the Grammar School and an Arts Centre. To the west of the town is the Pickaquoy Leisure Centre and cinema, with an adjacent, well appointed caravan and camp site.

Visitor Information

By Air

Kirkwall Airport
☎ 01856 886210
Situated in East Mainland, about 10 minutes out of town on the A960

Flybe
☎ 0871 700 2000
W: www.flybe.com

Loganair
☎ 01856 872494
W: www.flybe.com (as above)

By ferry to Kirkwall (Hatston)

Northlink Ferries from Aberdeen and Lerwick (Shetland)
☎ Reservations 0845 6000 449
E: info@northlinkferries.co.uk
Two to four sailings per week, depending upon the season
Also Scrabster (nr Thurso) to Stromness. Three

to four sailings daily depending on the season, much shorter sailing time (1½ hrs).

Pentland Ferries
Gills Bay to St Margaret's Hope, South Ronaldsay
☎ 01856 831226
E: sales@pentlandferries.co.uk
A 1 hour service with three to four sailings per day, (depending on season). A modern large catamaran carrying 32 cars, goods vehicles and up to 250 passengers.

John O'Groats Ferries
Passenger only service (40 mins) to Burwick in South Ronaldsay. Two to three times a day, May to end-September.
☎ 01955 611353
E: office@jogferry.co.uk

These ferries have connecting bus services to Kirkwall.

Orkney Tourist Guides Association
W: www.otga.co.uk

Kirkwall Visitor Information

Tourist Information: Visit Orkney
West Castle St., KW15 1GU
(by bus station)
☎ 01856 872856
Open: Apr-Sep, 8.30am-8pm; winter 9.30am-5pm; Mon-Sat
E: info@visitorkney.com

St Magnus Cathedral
Palace Road
☎ 01856 874894 to book upper floor tour.
Open: Apr-Sep, Mon-Sat 9am-6pm; Sun 1-6pm; winter, Mon-Sat 9am-1pm; 2-5pm.
Free admission.

Bishop's Palace
Watergate
☎ 01856 871918
Open: Apr-Sep, 9.30am-5.30pm; Oct, Sat-Wed 9.30am-4.30pm. Now a ruin.

Earl's Palace
Watergate
Opening times as the adjacent Bishop's Palace (joint ticket). Now a ruin.

St Magnus Centre
Palace Road, KW15 1PA
☎ 01856 878326
W: www.stmagnus.org/centre
Open: Apr-Sep, Mon-Sat 9.30am-5.30pm; Sunday 1.30-5.30pm; winter, Mon-Sat 12.30-2pm; closed Sunday.
Film about Cathedral and St Magnus. Free.

Orkney Museum
Tankerness House
Broad Street, KW15 1DH
☎ 01856 873535/873191
W: www.orkney.gov.uk/heritage
Open: May-Sep, Mon-Sat 10.30am-5pm; Oct-Apr, Mon-Sat 1.30-5pm
Free admission.

Highland Park Distillery
Holm Road, KW15 1SU
☎ 01856 874619
E: distillery@highlandpark.co.uk
Open: Apr-Sep, Mon-Fri 10am-5pm; May-Aug, Sat 10am-5pm; Sun 12-5pm; Oct-Mar, Mon-Fri 1-5pm. Tours hourly until 4pm in summer; winter earlier.

Swimming Pool and Sports Centre
☎ 01856 872364

Balfour Hospital/Health Centre
New Scarpa Road
☎ 01856 888000

Events

Annual County Show, early August.
Kirkwall Ba' game, Xmas day and 1st January, 1pm from the Cathedral.

Sands of Wright, Boys Ploughing match, South Ronaldsay, August
For a long list of all events in the islands go to W: www.visitorkney.com/events.

Island Ferries from Kirkwall

Orkney Ferries
☎ 01856 872004
To Whitehall (Stronsay); Loth (Sanday); Eday; North Ronaldsay; Westray (Peirowall and Rapness) and Papa Westray.

Other Ferries from West Mainland

Tingwall to Rousay, Wyre and Egilsay;
Stromness to Scrabster (near Thurso);
Stromness to Moaness (and via Graemsay);
Houton to Flotta; Houton to Hoy (Lyness); see also pp.11/12.

Camp/Caravan site

☎ 01856 879900
W: www.pickaquoy.co.uk
Situated adjacent to the Pickaquoy Leisure Centre/Cinema. The latter has facilities for children, plus bar/café. Fairly flat site with good facilities block (reception at the Leisure Centre).

Local Crafts

Various local crafts may be found for sale at the following mainland outlets. Look out for brown Craft Trail signs on roads.

Celina Rupp Jewellery

Orkney Wine Co, Lamb Holm Is.
☎ 01856 781770

Visit Orkney, Kirkwall

☎ 01856 872856
W: www.visitorkney.com
Ortak Jewellery, Halston Ind. Est. Kirkwall. ☎ 01856 872224

Pier Arts Centre

28-30 Victoria Street, Stromness
☎ 01856 850209
W: www.pierartscentre.com

Sheila Fleet Jewellery

30 Bridge Street. ☎ 01856 861203
W: www.sheilafleet.co.uk
Also at The Old School House, Tankerness

Skara Brae, Sandwick

☎ 01856 841815
W: www.historic-scotland.gov.uk

Skaill House, Sandwick

☎ 01856 841501
W: www.skaillhouse.co.uk

Tormiston Mill, Maeshowe

☎ 01856 761606
W: www.historic-scotland.gov.uk

Taxis

Kirkwall Taxis

☎ 01856 876972
Includes island tours.

Tour Guides

Wildabout Orkney

5 Clouston Corner, Stenness,
KW16 3LD
☎ 01856 851011

Orkney Archaeological Tours

☎ 01856 721217/721450

Discover Orkney Tours

☎ 01856 872865

Tour Orkney

Timetable information ☎ 0871 200 22 33.
Departs Kirkwall Travel Centre 10am. It visits Skara Brae, the Ring of Brodgar and The Italian Chapel.

West & East Mainland

Above: Maeshowe

Left: Tormiston Mill

Below: The Stones of Stenness

Top: Loch of Skaill
Middle: Skaill House
Bottom: The Skara Brae Visitor Centre

West Mainland

World Heritage Sites

Historic Scotland has in its care some of the finest archaeological sites in Europe. You can purchase an Explorer Pass if you propose visiting them all (or most of them, as access to the Brough of Birsay is controlled by the tide). There is a World Heritage Site Ranger Service if you would prefer a guided tour. ☎ 01856 841732. West Mainland has a fantastic concentration of Neolithic remains.

Adjacent to the Finstown – Stromness road (A965) is Tormiston Mill. Here you can not only look around the corn-mill but more importantly, buy timed tickets for Maeshowe, opposite. It looks to be no big deal, just a large mound in a field. Inside is another story altogether. At about 5,000 years old (or more), it was built some 1,500 years before Stonehenge. A low passageway leads to a corbelled-roofed chamber some 12ft/3.5m high. The size of many of the stones have to be seen to be believed and even more staggering is that many of the stones have been cut with stone implements, with the accuracy of a machine tool of today.

It was built so that the sun (if shining) on the winter solstice, 21st December, would shine up the entrance passage and strike the far side of the chamber. There are many Runic inscriptions (Viking graffiti). Equally impressive is the guide, who can read them. Maeshowe is the finest chambered tomb in Western Europe.

Just under a mile further on, turn right to the Stones of Stenness on your right. There are four standing stones here, with three of them together. They are huge and very impressive. Admission here is free. Also free but more impressive is the stone circle a further mile along the road. It is the Ring of Brodgar. Originally with some 60 stones arranged vertically, it still retains 27 of them, with others lying on the ground. The ring overlooks Harray Loch with 3,000acres/1,214hecs of brown trout freshwater fishing. At nearby Ness of Brodgar, a Neolithic Cathedral was uncovered in 2009. It is unique in Britain and is some 65ft/20m in length and width, with walls 16ft/5m thick. Walls are up to 3ft/1m in height; but note limited access only.

To the north-west and right on the coast, is Skara Brae, with its preserved 5,000 year old village and new visitor centre. The village is of similar age to Maeshowe. A recreation of a village 'house' and its covered stone-lined access is worth going into, as the original buildings were taller than they are today. This is a large site and you can wander around, looking down into the buildings from the pathways. The houses can still be seen with their stone furniture intact. Adjacent is Skaill House, a 17th century mansion, also open to the public.

To the north is Brough Head on the island of Brough of Birsay. It has a causeway access, which is uncovered for a couple of hours either side of low tide. It is worth the trip (on foot) across to it (watch the times of the tides). It has Pictish and Norse settlements plain to see (and close to the causeway) and the remains of an 11th century church. Tide tables are available at Skara Brae. Look out for the cast of a Pictish carved stone.

At Birsay, on the mainland nearby, is The Earls Palace, built in 1574. The

Palace is quite extensive and was built by Robert, Earl of Orkney. By 1700 it was little used, however. It was built with four wings (but only three corner towers), around a courtyard. Adjacent is the small St Magnus's Church, established in 1064AD, but the current building is of a much more recent date.

Proceeding back towards Finstown and Kirkwall on the A966, the road runs close to Eynhallow Sound and Eynhallow Island. About a mile after the B9057 goes off to Dounby, there is a turning to the left just before the Community Centre. This takes you down to the Broch of Gurness. Some maps show an earlier route left to the Broch, but ignore it as it includes a long length of rough unmade track. The Broch is quite large but without its tower. It dates from c. first century BC and is unusual in that it clearly had a large settlement between it and its defensive ditch. Much of it survives and the whole site is quite impressive and its coastal situation quite spectacular.

There is another broch, equally spectacular, but with a smaller surrounding settlement, across Eynhallow Sound on Rousay Island. That site, however, has another ace up its proverbial sleeve: the largest chambered tomb in the country. It is called Mid Howe (see p.44).

For a fascinating overview of these impressive Neolithic remains – and many more nearby which are unexcavated (or excavated but with no reports of finds) – the Historic Scotland guide *Maeshowe and the Heart of Neolithic Orkney* is recommended. There used to be several brochs on either side of the Sound, which must have been an impressive sight.

Woodland Walks

Orkney is not well wooded. However, the Orkney Woodland Projects has produced a free leaflet on six woodland walks, one at Kirkwall, three in West Mainland, one in East Mainland and one on Hoy. The latter is Berriedale Wood, the most northerly relict wood in the British Isles. Over 120 new woodlands have been planted for the future during the period of 1998-2009.

Exploring West Mainland

Having looked at the Broch of Gurness, a perambulation of West Mainland is recommended and it is picked up at Birsay. Here, if tides are right (take no risks if not, check with the Tourist Information Office first), you can walk across to the small island of Brought of Birsay, where the puffins and other seabirds will no doubt fascinate you. Keep an eye open on the coastline and out to sea for seals and even the larger mammals up to whales. There are Pictish and Viking remains on the island.

In Birsay is another ruined Earl's Palace dating from the 16th century, but two other properties of interest are still complete: St. Magnus's Church of 1760 and Boardhouse Mill. The church may be on a religious site going back to the Viking period and where St. Magnus was originally interred after being murdered in 1116 AD. His remains were later removed to Kirkwall Cathedral.

The watermill is the only surviving watermill on Orkney still producing meal and open to visitors. It was built in

Above left: House at Skara Brae

Mid-left: recreated house and view of site

Above: Boardhouse Mill, Birsay

Below: The Earl's Palace, Birsay

Opposite top: The Broch of Gurness

Mid-left: the main street, Stromness

Mid-right: waterfront properties with the nearest housing the museum, Stromness

Opposite bottom: early morning mist rising at Stromness

1873. Not too far away, is the Click Mill, Orkney's only horizontal waterwheel driven mill. To reach it, take the A967 from Birsay towards Stromness, then left on the A986 to Dounby. Turn left here on the B905 for 2 miles/3km and the mill is on the right.

Above the Khartoum cliffs and a little further south of Birsay is a monument to Lord Kitchener who died aboard *HMS Hampshire* in 1916. All the crew were killed except for twelve fortunate men. A German mine is cited as the cause, but the disaster was hushed up at the time because of interest in why Kitchener was on board. It is believed that he was on a secret mission to Russia. The tall monument can be seen from many vantage points.

At least the views from here are memorable, above high cliffs. Kitchener remains in the memory of most of us for his face on the 'Britain Needs You' poster during the Great War recruitment campaign. He was not a popular man at the time with other politicians but was a war hero himself, respected by the men under him throughout a distinguished career. 'K of K', as he was known, had even wrestled Khartoum back, after a two year campaign, following the death of General Gordon. He was Secretary of State for War at the time of his death.

Inland from Birsay is Kirbuster Farm Museum. Dating from the early 19th century, it has the island's last central hearth, still fired by peat (in the original way), stone beds, plus a collection of old agricultural implements. It is an important link with the island's vernacular architecture, stretching back centuries.

There is another farm museum at Corrigall, to the left of the A986, on the road to Finstown from Birsay Bay (road initially designated the A967). It is the Orkney Farm and Folklore Museum. However the road to continue a circumnavigation of West Mainland runs south as the B9056 to Skaill and Skara Brae, mentioned above. From here it is the best part of 10 miles/16km to Stromness, initially on the B9056 and then on the A967. Stromness is Orkney's second town. This busy seaport (ferry to Scrabster on the Scottish mainland) is the main port in the Orkneys and has a distinctive layout, rising up from the sea front with narrow streets and buildings erected gable-on to the street. Many of the streets are too narrow for vehicles and seen from the sea they create a view where houses seem to be sitting on the one below. There is a Tourist Information Centre here, plus a Museum covering connections with the sea, local wildlife etc. The Pier Arts Centre has an important collection of modern paintings gifted to Orkney (including by Barbara Hepworth, Ben Nicholson and others).

Stromness is a fascinating place to explore. Its main street is a series of different named streets one a continuation of another. All are paved with stone with no side pavements. There are many narrow streets or passages leading off, one (with the library on the corner) called Hellyhole and another Khyber Pass.

Look out for signs giving historical information about particular properties. Some are fascinating, especially the one at Mrs Humphrey's House, Alfred Street which tells you of it being used in 1835-36 to care for whalers suffering from scurvy after being trapped in ice for months. You pass the museum en-route and emerge a little short of the promontory and golf club. Here too is a coastal path and a good camping and caravanning site at Ness.

Stromness is a fascinating place to visit. It has kept its historic properties and its identity. It is all the better for it too. It contrasts strongly with the modern ferry terminal and its huge ferry boats gliding relatively silently in and out on the Scrabster run.

From Stromness, the A964 leads you back to Kirkwall, around the lovely Bay of Ireland and around the northern side of Scapa Flow. Much of the interior of West Mainland is covered by water, particularly the Loch of Harray and the neighbouring Loch of Strenness, with a succession of other, smaller lochs to the north. It is a great area to visit if you have a love of birds.

Visitor Information

Earl's Palace
Birsay, open all year (free)
Boardhouse Mill, Birsay
☎ 01856 721439
E: miller@birsay.org.uk
Open: 10-1pm and 2-5pm, daily, 1May–30 Sept. Free

Corrigall Farm Museum
☎ 01856 771411
Open: Mar-Oct, Mon-Sat 10.30am-1pm and 2-5pm; Sun 12-5pm. Free

Kirbuster Museum
Open: Mar-Oct, Mon-Sat 10.30am-1pm and 2-5pm; Sun 12-5pm. Free

RSPB Birsay Moors
☎ 018560 850176
E: orkney@rspb.org.uk
Over 5,500acres/2,226hecs of moorland. Site is near Evie.

RSPB Marwick Head
Contact: see RSPB Birsay Moors
Spectacular seacliffs & seabird colonies close to Kitchener's monument.

RSPB The Loons & Loch of Banks
Contact: see RSPB Birsay Moors
Wetland species/hide. Situated NW of Loch of Ibister, South of Birsay.

Tormiston Mill
☎ 01856 761606
Open as for Maeshowe

Maeshowe
☎ 01856 761606
Open: 9.30-5pm; winter to 4pm. Tickets from Tormiston Mill

Skara Brae
☎ 01856 841815

Broch of Gurness
☎ 01856 751414
Open: Apl-Sept, 9.30-12.30/1.30-5pm
Oct - Sat-Wed only, 9.30-4pm

The Woolshed
Benlaw, Costa KW17 2NN
☎ 01856 751305
W: www.woolshed-orkney.co.uk
Traditional stone longhouse and attached kiln. Includes N. Ronaldsay fleeces.

Fursbreck Pottery
Harray KW172JR
☎ 01856 771419
Also smoked delicacies; mail order available.
W: www.applesmoke.co.uk

Orkneyinga Saga Centre & Round Church
Orphir
Open daily, free

Schoolquoy Garden
Scorradale Road, KW17 2RF
☎ 01856 811293
Open: Jun-Aug, Thurs-Mon 12noon-5pm; closed Tues, Wed
Garden and tearoom.

Top left: Old Mill, Whitecleat, Tankerness; *Top right:* Exhibit at Tomb of The Eagles
Above: The Orkney Fossil & Heritage Centre, Burray

St Margaret's Hope waterfront

Above: Hunda Island, off Burray, with Churchill Barrier and Scarpa Flow

Below: Newark Bay, East Mainland

Appie's Tearoom & Gallery
Lower Applehouse,
Sandwick KW15 3JD
☎ 01856 841562
W: www.pamfarmer.co.uk

Stromness

Visit Orkney Information Centre
Stromness Travel Centre
Pier Head, Stromness KW16 1BH
☎ 01856 850716
W: www.stromness @visitorkney.com

Argo's Bakery
50 Victoria Street, KW163BS
☎ 01856 850245
Locally produced products.

Northlight
☎ 01856 850671

Graham Place
Gallery & tapestry studio, short courses
available.

Pier Arts Centre
☎ 01856 850209
W: www.pierartscentre.com
Open: Mon-Sat, 10.30am--5pm; also Sun
May-Sep. Free Admission.

Quernstone Knitwear
41 Victoria Street
☎ 01856 852900
W: www.quernstone.co.uk
Locally made products.

W S Sindair Fishing Tackle
27 John Street
☎ 01856 851523

Stromness Books & Prints
1 Graham Place
☎ 01856 850565

Stromness Museum
52 Alfred Street
☎ 01856 850025
Open: daily Apr-Sep, 10am-5pm; Oct-Mar,
Mon-Sat 11am-3.30pm

Waterfront Gallery
128 Victoria Street
☎ 01856 850644

Activities

Orkney Cycle Hire
54 Dundas Street
☎ 01856 850255
W: www.orkneycyclehire.co.uk

Scapa Scuba
PADI Dive Centre
☎ 01856 851218
W: www.scapascuba.co.uk

Golf Club
☎ 01856 850772
W: www.stromnessgc.co.uk
18 holes, Par 65, 4,882yds; clubs for hire,
fees payable at clubhouse.

Aurora
Old Finstown Road, St Ola KW15 1TP
☎ 01856 871861 Orkney jewellery.

Swimming Pool
☎ 01856 850552

East Mainland

To the east of Kirkwall is a smallish area
(relative to West Mainland) consisting
of three parishes: two in the north, St.
Andrews and Deerness, plus Holm in
the south, with a dissected coastline, the
area stretches roughly 12m/19km west
to east and 10m/16km from north to
south. It is largely agricultural. To the
east are the islands of Cain Holm and
Copinsay. To the south lies the Churchill
Barrier, Lamb Holm and the islands to
the south, all linked by the Churchill
Barrier Causeway, built to guard the
eastern approach to Scarpa Flow. The
area offers good views from the coast
and houses Orkney's airport. It is 3-4
miles/5-6km south-east of Kirkwall on

the A960. A narrow neck of land, with Kirkwall at its northern end divides East Mainland from the much larger area of West Mainland. To the south lay Britain's safest naval refuge, until a German U-Boat in a brazen example of revenge, forced a passage to sink the *HMS Royal Oak*, in 1939 with a huge loss of over 800 men. Retribution one suspects for the loss of the German Navy here; scuttled in a final act of defiance by the Kaiser's Navy at the end of the Great War.

Of interest are several beaches and cliffs, including the collapsed sea cave called The Gloup. Amazingly, when the sea cave roof collapsed, a section remained as a land-bridge. It is on the east side of the Deerness peninsula. Adjacent is the Mull Head Nature Reserve, with 200 acres of protected heath, grassland and cliff with a large seabird colony. Perhaps the loveliest beach is Newark Bay. Also on Mull Head is the Covenanters Memorial of 1888 erected to mark where over 200 Covenanters were drowned in 1679. They were on a prison ship bound for America. The ship was wrecked and although the crew escaped, only 50 or so Covenanters escaped assisted by just one of the sailors.

Nearby on the Brough of Deerness are the remains of a Viking chapel and rectangular buildings, but access is via a steep and narrow path requiring care.

Mentioned above is the island of Copinsay, a small island with impressive cliffs. It, along with adjacent even smaller islands, composes the James Fisher Memorial Reserve of the RSPB. Some 4,500 kittewakes and 20,000 guillemots nest here. It is visible from the south-east coast of East Mainland.

Visitor Information

Sheila Fleet Jewellery
Tankerness
☎ 01856 861203
W: www.sheila-fleet.co.uk
Designers and producers of gold and silver jewellery.

RSPB, Copinsay Island
Restricted access only

Mull Head Nature Reserve
Leaflet from TICs

Mine Howe Iron Age Chamber
St. Mary's
☎ 01856 861209
Mine Howe has 29 steps down to an Iron Age site. It is all underground. There are two cabins at the side of the road opposite the cemetery, which act as reception.
Unusual structure with interpretative display.

South Ronaldsay & The Southern Islands

This island is the nearest part of the Orkneys to mainland Scotland. It is situated 6½ miles/10km from John O'Groats and there is a direct ferry link to the island (to St. Margaret's Hope) from Gill's Bay in Caithness (west of John O'Groats). South Ronaldsay is connected to the mainland of Orkney by the Churchill Barriers, built after the loss of *HMS Royal Oak* in 1939. The four Barriers closed off the east approach and after the war, causeways were created between Holm on the Orkney mainland and the islands of Lamb Holm, Glimps Holm, Burray and finally South Ronaldsay.

Italian Chapel interior

Left: Italian Chapel

Above: Sunken blockship on the Churchill Barrier No.3

Below: Sands of Wright and Hoxa. South Ronaldsay

Top: Blockship at Burray

Above: Scarpa Flow from Hoy. The German fleet was anchored mainly beyond Ryse Little Island on the right and around Cava Island beyond. Wideford Hill on the far right

Left: Fishing boat at the northern end of Barrier 3 at Glimps Holm

The main community is St. Margaret's Hope. Like Burray to the north, the island draws ornithologists like a magnet and whilst Burray has good water sports facilities on offer, both are a good base to seek out the birds or for diving on the clear waters of Scarpa Flow. Here are the remaining seven hulks of the Great War German High Seas Fleet, scuttled to prevent the Royal Navy from using them, plus the *Royal Oak*, now an official war grave, with its site clearly marked. With clear, unpolluted water, Scarpa Flow is a popular diving venue described as being one of the best in Europe. Diving, however, is not permitted on *HMS Royal Oak*.

At the end of the causeway is the Orkney Fossil and Heritage Centre. There is much to see, including recreated house rooms, some rare local fossils, the community café and gift shop.

To the west of Burray is the small island of Hunda. This too has a causeway, an extension of the Churchill Barriers. The island is unhabited but there is a path around the island from which the bird colonies may be viewed and of course, the seals and other mammals which frequent the coastal waters. If you do go to Hunda, please call at Little Quoy Farm just before the causeway to inform them of your intentions. The island is still grazed and care needs to be taken with the stock.

On South Ronaldsay, St. Margaret's Hope (the third largest town on Orkney after Kirkwall and Stromness) has hotels, a restaurant described by Visit Orkney as 'first class', cafés, shops etc. (Burray offers similar facilities, not forgetting several nice sandy beaches too).

The Sands of Wright is a large popular beach on the road to Hoxa. In addition to the annual boys' ploughing match each August, there is a short circular walk through wetlands alongside a loch and back to the roadside beach parking area. At Hoxa look out for the wartime batteries built to defend Scarpa Flow. You may have seen these from the ferry to St Margaret's Hope. Craft Trail signs lead you to the Tapestry Gallery and there is another Craft shop in Front Road, St Margaret's Hope.

The ferry from Gills Bay, near John O'Groats, docks at St Margaret's Hope, a little way out of the village. A pedestrian ferry (only) operates from John O'Groats to Burwick at the southern end of South Ronaldsay. There is a Tourist Information Centre at St Margaret's Hope, but it is up Back Road and not down by the village centre. The main tourist attraction on South Ronaldsay is the Tomb of the Eagles, to the east of Burwick. Here you can see finds (there is a good interpretation centre), and learn about them and the people that built the tomb. You can also explore the latter which is about 15 minutes away. The finds uncovered here were both numerous and important.

Travelling north via the causeways, you will pass a sign to the right on Lambs Holm Island to the Italian Chapel. It is usually open and was built in 1943 by Italian POW during WWII from a couple of Nissan huts. It was adjacent to the camp of which foundations remain. It is beautiful inside, well worth the visit and remains a House of God.

Visitor Information

By road from the Orkney mainland and by sea from Gill's Bay, Caithness (on the Scottish mainland) and from John O'Groats to Burwick. See p. 12.

Halcro Head

South East Coast

A scenic coastal path which leads from the Tomb of the Eagles (see below). There is a gloup (blow hole) at Halcro Head.

Harrabrough

on the West Coast.

Large cliffs and natural arch. Avoid the cliff edge.

Hoxa Head

Waymarked path, noted for its flora. Several coastal battery sites.

Tomb of the Eagles

Liddle, S. Ronaldsay
☎ 01856 831339
W: www.tomboftheeagles.co.uk
Open: Apr-Oct, 9.30am-5.30pm; Mar 10am-12 noon; other times by arrangement, craft shop, café.
Impressive chambered tomb situated in the far south-east, near Liddle Farm, dates from c. 3000 BC. Named after quantities of eagle bones were found here and the burial site of c. 340 people. A total of 16,000 human and animal bones were found here.

Italian Chapel

On the north side of Lamb Holm Island.
☎ 01856 781268
Free admission

Old St. Mary's Church

One of the oldest chapels in Scotland Key held nearby. West of Tomb of the Eagles
☎ 01856 831212

Orkney Fossil and Heritage Centre

Viewforth, Burray
☎ 01856 731255
W: www.orkneyfossilcentre.co.uk
Open: Apr-Sep, 10am-4pm; June-Aug 10am-5pm

Smiddy Museum

Cromarty Square
St Margaret's Hope
☎ 01856 831497
Restored blacksmith's shop.
Open: May-Sep or by appointment.
Free admission.

Boy's Ploughing Match

Sands of Wright
August

Local Crafts

The Workshop & Loft Gallery
Front Road, St Margaret's Hope
☎ 01856 831587
Open: Mon-Sat, 10am-5pm

Hoxa Tapestry Gallery

Neviholm, Hoxa, St Margaret's Hope KW17 2TW
☎ 01856 831395

Watersound Gallery

Burray
☎ 01856 731543
W: www.briancollier.co.uk
Open: Sun-Fri, 2-5pm

Hoy Island

The other large island to the south of the mainland is Hoy, which borders the western side of Scarpa Flow. It is the second largest island in the Orkney Islands and covers 57 sq miles/148 sqkm. It extends some 13 miles/21km in length and 6 miles/10km wide. It also has the Orkney's highest hill, Ward Hill, which is 1,570ft/479m in height from the sea, making the island's profile look like a couple of whale humps. Situated at the northern end of Hoy,

Above: The Old Man of Hoy

Below: Summer colours, looking east to Scarpa Flow, Hoy

Above left: The ferry leaving Flotta for Hoy (from Houton); *Above right:* The northern hills, Hoy; *Above:* Burnmouth, Rackwick, Hoy; *Below left:* Longhope, Hoy; *Below right:* World War II Naval Gun, Lyness, Hoy

this part of the island is the upland part, with the south and eastern areas being comparatively low lying. The 9,500 acre/3845hec RSPB North Hoy Nature Reserve covers much of the north end of the island. There is some good hill walking in the north, including at least a three hour round trip from Rackwick to visit Orkney's most well known landmark, the Old Man of Hoy. It is a 5.5 miles/9km round trip from Rackwick on foot. Rising 450 ft/136m this slender column of stone was first climbed in 1966 and was televised live over a couple of days or so. It is the highest sea stack in Britain and can be viewed from the Stromness-Scabster ferry. This area is the Highlands of Orkney. In fact Ward Hill is the highest point of Great Britain north of the Pentland Firth.

The ferry for vehicles leaves Houton, south-west of Kirkwall, crossing Scarpa Flow to Lyness on the south-east side of Hoy. The ferry may well call at Flotta Island on the way, calling at the pier by the oil terminal. Lyness is about 15 minutes further on. There is also a passenger ferry only (no vehicles) from Stromness to Moaness Pier at the north end of the island. It is essential to remember that there is no public transport on Hoy.

Lyness was the main centre for the Royal Navy when Scarpa Flow was used as an anchorage in the two World Wars, guarding the North Atlantic shipping lanes. It was here that U-47 sneaked in undetected and sunk *HMS Royal Oak* under the Admiralty's nose in 1939. Here too, the German High Seas Fleet was scuttled in 1919 by German crews, sending 52 vessels to the bottom They were raised by marine salvage expert Ernest Cox, mainly for scrap

(see page 36).

Today the area around Lyness retains many of its military buildings, quite a few in ruins, some with other uses. The Scarpa Flow Visitor Centre is opposite the pier and is unmistakeable with its naval guns pointing to the sea. By the ferry terminal are the remains of two naval jetties dating from the Great War.

Up the road is the flat-roofed Hoy Hotel, one of three hotels on the island and equally one of three places serving evening meals and drinks. The other two are at Longhope. The latter is on the former island of South Walls, connected to Hoy by a causeway (The Ayre) in the early years of the 20th century. Although only a couple of hundred yards/metres from the road on Hoy, there is a long detour around the bay on the B9047 to get there. Longhope has two hotels, The Royal and The Stromabank. The latter is on the hill out of town and with superb views from its dining room. The well-stocked general store of John M F Groat & Sons on the pier also sells petrol/diesel (at about 15% above mainland prices) and camping gas. Longhope also has a health centre, beyond the pier and an RNLI shop by the general store.

A couple of miles along the road, beyond Longhope, you will reach Martello Tower and Hackness Battery, now under Historic Scotland's guardianship. This large diameter stone-built fortress dates from c. 1815 and is one of two which were built to protect local shipping, chiefly from the French. It retains a cannon on top of it.

At the beginning of the causeway to South Walls a turn to the right along the south side of Aith Hope takes you past the first Longhope lifeboat station, a small stone-built building dating from 1874 and in use until 1906. It was then replaced by the station with the slip down into the sea further along the coast and closed in 1999. The latter building is now the home of the Longhope Trust. It houses a former Longhope lifeboat, the *Thomas McCunn*, which served the station from 1933-62. The current lifeboat is kept in Longhope Harbour. It was from here that the *T.G.B.*, was launched on that fateful day in 1969 (see p.35).

Proceeding north from Longhope towards Lyness, you pass the Gable End Theatre in the former school. North of Lyness, the road hugs the coast for a while before heading directly uphill across the moors towards Hoy village. Close to the shore are the islands of Fara and then Rysa with Cava rising behind it. It was around these islands, especially Cava that the German High Seas Fleet was moored in 1919.

On the way, look out for Betty Corrigall's grave. A plaque tells you why she was buried here. Just before Hoy, a road goes off to the left to Rackwick. On the way look out for the sign pointing left to the path to Dwarfie Stone, clearly visible on the hillside on the far side of the valley. Rackwick is a collection of crofts situated above an attractive bay, with a backcloth of two high hills. The views are memorable. In the bay, the Hoy Trust has a bothy at Burnmouth, where the stream reaches the sea. Above the village is Rackwick Youth Hostel with its adjacent campsite. The Burnmouth bothy is free to use.

One of the original crofts is now the Crow's Nest Museum. To the north of Rackwick is Berriedale Wood, the most northerly relict woodland in Britain. The area has many plant species which are rare or unknown elsewhere in the islands. A little further to the north is St. John's Head, the highest vertical sea cliff in Britain at 1,128 ft./335m Take a midge net with you!

Visitor Information

Orkney Ferries
Shore Street, Kirkwall, Orkneys KW15 1LG
☎ 01856 872004/0800 011 3648
E: info@orkneyferries.co.uk
Passenger only ferry, Stromness–Hoy (Moaness); calls at Graemsay and takes 25 minutes. Houton–Flotta/Hoy (Lyness)

Places to Visit

Crow's Nest, Rackwick
☎ 01856 791262
Traditional croft house

Dwarfie Stone
A remarkable prehistoric rock tomb, between Quoys and Rackwick. Hollowed out of a huge block of standstone, 28ft/8½m long. Thought to be 5,000 years old.

Swimming Pool, North Walls
☎ 01856 701460

Graemsay Island
Small island with sandy beach, island covered in flowers in summer.
Ferry from Moaness in North Hoy (see above).

Hoy Kirk, Hoy village
☎ 01856 791098
Audio-visual presentations.

Longhope Lifeboat Station (Longhope Trust)
Brims, South Walls KW16 3PG
☎ 01856 701332
E: info@longhopelifeboat.org.uk
Now a museum (free entry)

Scarpa Flow Visitor Centre, Lyness

☎ 01856 791300

E: scarpaflow@orknet.co.uk

Records the Royal Navy in Orkney during two World Wars. Has a café.

Martello Tower/Longhope Battery

Longhope

☎ 01856 701727

Open: Apr-Sep, 9.30am-5.30pm; Oct, 9.30am-4.30pm

Flotta

This slumbering island is now of importance economically for it houses an important oil terminal, receiving the oil from the Piper Platform. It was also important during the two World Wars because of its location in Scarpa Flow. The island claims to have one of the finest panoramas in Britain, There are fine views over Scarpa Flow. The Buchanan Battery on Flotta was built to defend the main entrance into this natural harbour, being south of the main area of Scarpa Flow. It has an airstrip built to facilitate construction of the oil terminal. Flotta means flat, which describes the island's form.

The ferry docks at the pier outside the gates to the oil terminal.

The attack on HMS Royal Oak

A few days after the start of World War II, on the night of October 13-14ᵗʰ 1939, a German submarine penetrated the defences of Scarpa Flow and sunk *HMS Royal Oak*, with the loss of 833 men. The Flow had a reputation for being impregnable, with booms and block-ships covering the various entrances. However, the Admiralty had repeatedly been told of points of weakness, especially between the island chain on the east-side. Block-ships had been sunk between these islands which had intensified the currents which flowed in or out of the Flow depending upon the state of the tide. However, it was still possible to navigate through and German trawlers had been seen doing so before the war.

Perhaps the weakest place was Kirk Sound just to the north of Lamb Holm and where the Italian Chapel is now situated. Two more block-ships had been ordered by the Admiralty and one had been placed a few days before the attack. The second, which would have sealed Kirk Sound, arrived and was placed the day after the attack.

The latter came from a submarine, *U-47*, commanded by Lt. Gunther Prien. Having run the gauntlet and succeeded in reaching the prized waters of the Flow, against all expected odds, he found the anchorage largely devoid of targets. *HMS Repulse*, *HMS Renown* and *HMS Hood*, for example, had recently left for an exercise and sent elsewhere, for fears of an air attack.

German aerial intelligence was a few days old, but Prien found *HMS Royal Oak* just off the coast north of St Mary's. She was an ageing Great War veteran, close to retirement, having been built in 1916. Of the first wave of four torpedoes, three missed or were duds. Three of the next four took the ship to the bottom. Only 424 men survived out of a compliment of 1,257. She keeled over and went down in 13 minutes.

Having prized open the Flow's back door and emblazoned his name in infamy (from the British perspective), *U-47* then made it back out to open sea and back to Germany, where Prien was honoured by Hitler.

Today the wreck is a war-grave, lying upside down on her superstructure. Each year, Navy divers place a wreath on the upturned keel. The full story is told in *Nightmare at Scarpa Flow* by H J Weaver, which is recommended and is available widely in Orkney.

The Longhope Lifeboat Disaster

At the southern end of Hoy Island, there is a broad inlet of Scarpa Flow known as the Aith Hope. It stretches to the community of Longhope, which had had a lifeboat station since 1874. Its honour-board is distinguished with its lifeboat men being tested in critical times over the years since then. Many of us, one feels, are quietly in awe of men who go to sea in times of dire need and danger, risking all in the hands of Providence, good luck and supreme seamanship. The ultimate test falls thankfully on only a few occasions compared to the many call-outs there are in all. However, for some crews, that test pits brave men to the ultimate challenge in huge and unforgiving seas. Such a challenge was visited upon the Longhope crew in March 1969.

The Longhope men had a 47ft, Watson class lifeboat called the *T.G.B.*

She received the coastguard call of a service to attend upon a 2,000-ton Liberian ship, *The Irene* said to be in distress, but actually nowhere near her stated position. She had apparently run out of fuel. The eight men crew launched from the lighthouse, built in 1906, and now the home of the Longhope Memorial Trust. On board were the coxswain David Kirkpatrick and his two sons Daniel and John. The second cox was James Johnson, on board with his father Robert (the lifeboat's mechanic) and his brother, Robert. The assistant mechanic was James Swanson and finally, but not least, there was crew member Eric McFadden.

The Watson class lifeboat had a shelter for the crew and as the coxswain was out in the open (and often wet through), he was usually lashed to the wheel in bad weather. The boat was out in a Force 9 gale with 60ft/20m high waves, heading for a ship which did not exist at the given location. A TV programme on extreme weather has suggested that the boat may have been overcome by a freak 100ft/30m high wave. The *T.G.B.* was located 4 miles/6km south-west of the south-west tip of Hoy at 1.40pm the following day and was towed upside down to Scrabster. All of the crew bar James Swanson were still on board.

They were buried at Osmondwell church, Kirkhope, where a bronze statue was erected; the Queen Mother unveiled a plaque at Walls church. The *Irene's* crew survived, being driven ashore near Grimness, in the north-east of South Ronaldsay. Today the *T.G.B.* may be seen at the Scottish Maritime Museum at Irvine, South Ayrshire. The tragedy led to the development of a self-righting boat.

The Scarpa Flow Scuttle of the German Fleet

Military action in the Great War ended on the 11th hour of the 11th day of the 11th month of 1918. War had not ended, but an Armistice had begun and it lasted over a year. The German High Seas Fleet had been conspicuous by its absence during the hostilities with the exception of the Battle of Jutland. Britain and her Allies demanded reparations and as part of that demanded 74 vessels of the High Seas Fleet as 'security'. To persuade Germany to accept this, Britain threatened to invade Heligoland in the southern North Sea, the last thing the Germans wanted and were powerless to stop.

This is how 74 vessels set sail from Germany for a neutral or British port. Britain had other ideas, they were going to Scarpa Flow for internment (not that the word was uttered). Once there, each vessel was isolated, with no trips to land or to other vessels. Even the German naval flag could not be raised let alone a signal or use of other communication between vessels or to elsewhere, eg Germany.

However, supplies had to be sent from Germany and so some contact with the homeland was possible. Tension grew in December 1919 as the final date for the end of the Armistice came ever nearer. Would it be peace or back to the fighting? Would Britain seize the High Seas Fleet as soon as the Armistice ended with no Peace Agreement? Would it do this if the Peace Treaty had been signed but not ratified in time, which seemed likely?

In the event the Commander of the German Interned Fleet, Vice Admiral von Reuter, decided the decision was his and his alone. Reacting to British newspaper reports (which were four days old) he decided to scuttle his fleet on 21st June 1919. Fifty-two vessels went to the bottom, with quite a few beached in time by the British. Over 400,000-tons of prime warship technology, some of the finest naval vessels afloat were lost. The British, however, did not need the ships. Rationalisation of the British fleet was not far off. The Germans had removed one of the world's finest fleets from play at a stroke. Even the Royal Navy couldn't have too many qualms over that.

Today, post-Hiroshima and Nagasaki's nuclear fallout, all modern steel is tainted with radiation. The seven ships remaining on the bottom are one of the largest concentrations of non-radiation affected steel in the world. The rest have been raised, many by the formidable Ernest Cox, who even brought up some heavy ships in 90 seconds. Only recently has his record of bringing up the heaviest ship from the bottom (26,000 tons in 1930), in the form of the Hindenburg, been broken. A plaque recording this achievement is attached to the waiting room at Lyness harbour, for the 70th anniversary of it being raised in 1930.

Recommended reading: The Grand Scuttle, by Dan Van Der Vat, widely available on Orkney.

Scarpa Flow fortifications on South Ronaldsay

Getting There

North of Orkney mainland are various islands, the main ones being served by ferry and six also having an airport. It is not possible to island hop by ferry. Vessels run from Tingwall (west mainland) to Rousay, Wyre and Egilsay; Kirkwall to Shapinsay; Kirkwall to Stronsay, Eday and Sanday; Kirkwall to Westray, Papa Westray and North Ronaldsay. Exceptionally on a couple of Sundays in summer, it is possible to get a ferry from Stronsay to North Ronaldsay (both ways) and from Eday and Sanday to Westray/Papa Westray (both ways) and from Sanday to North Ronaldsay (both ways).

By Air

Loganair have scheduled flights from Kirkwall to Stronsay, Eday, Sanday, Westray, Papa Westray and North Ronaldsay. Senior citizens discounts are available for the over 60s on many full economy fares (except to North Ronaldsay and Papa Westray and on certain other flights). If you stay overnight on these two islands there is a reduced price to the islands. Also concessions for the under 17s to these islands.

Shapinsay

Situated 4m/6km north east of Kirkwall, it is generally flat with Ward Hill rising to 210ft/64m in height, from where there are good panoramic views over the whole of the Orkney Islands. It is 6 miles/9km in length. With a population of c. 300 (769 in 1901), the island is well served by the Orkney car ferry from Kirkwall to Balfour. If there is space, use the long stay car park left of the toilets and Orkney Ferries offices, on the Kirkwall waterfront. Agriculture and tourism fuel the local economy. A feature of the island are several ayres, fresh water lakes created by a sand spit sealing off a part of the sea. Gradual desalination occurs and the areas are popular with waders and seabirds.

Dominating Balfour as you arrive are the turrets of Balfour Castle. The former home of the Balfour family, who owned the island, it was built in 1782 as Cliffdale House, but was extended in Scottish Baronial style in Victorian times. It dominates the village, which housed estate workers in former times.

Now the castle gate house, a massive structure in itself, is the island's pub. Other facilities nearby include a shop, petrol station and a post office. The former two-storey smithy is now the Shapinsay Heritage Centre, incorporating the island's craftshop and an archive display. Another building is Elwick Mill, a large water-powered grinding mill now used as a pottery.

Upon arrival, the main street consists of a long terrace of single-storey houses, built by the Balfours for estate workers. At the end of the street is the home farm. Productivity was enhanced here by bringing the island's best soils to it, at the expense of tenant farmers! At the end of this street turn right, past the

Round Tower, the remaining piece of the 1851 gas works. You then pass the Community School, turning left for Mill Dam RSPB Reserve and reaching Elwick Mill on your left.

If you turned left for Mill Dam, RSPB reserve, note that there is no access to the reserve, but to a hide which is open daily and without charge. There are many species of water fowl and waders, plus the water rail (if you are lucky!). In winter, these residents are joined by large quantities of ducks, geese and whooper swans.

Two structures worth seeking out are the Burroughston Broch, in the north east of the island. Close to the seashore, it has a big ditch and rampart, with quite a bit of the structure below ground level, but open to view. It is impressive and allows you to see how it was built and used. The coast nearby offers good opportunities to observe seals at close quarters. A couple of miles away near Linton Bay is Linton Chapel which dates from c. 12th century. Closer to the broch is Quoime (on the opposite side of the peninsula). Here lived the father of Washington Irving. Never heard of him? You've probably heard of his book: *Rip Van Winkle*.

Visitor Information

Orkney Ferries from Kirkwall to Balfour, taking about half an hour, from Kirkwall Pier in Shore Streeet

Balfour Castle Hotel
☎ 01856 711282
E: info@balfourcastle.co.uk

Orkney Island Holidays
Furrowend, Shapinsay K17 2DY
☎ 01856 711373

E: holidays@orkney.com
Guided tours of wildlife and archaeology.

Groat's Tours
Fishing trips with B&B (also staying in the castle available).
☎ 01856 711254
W: www.orkneyangling.co.uk

Shapinsay Heritage Centre, Balfour
☎ 01856 711258
Open daily, noon – 4.30pm (later on Wed and Sun)

Mill Dam RSPB Reserve
Open daily; free.

Events

Shapinsay Agricultural Show
early August

Produced locally are Orkney Preserves, Odinstone, Shapinsay. KW17 2DZ
☎ 01856 711389

Rousay, Egilsay and Wyre

Just off the Orkney mainland north east coast are these three small islands. Despite the diminutive size of them, collectively they encompass the unique heritage of Orkney – to quote 'Visit Orkney'. It is no exaggeration for remains of culture stretching from the Stone Age to today may be seen. However, it is not just the 5,500 years of history which is impressive. These three tiny islands shelter over 166 sites of archaeological interest. If that was not enough, these include some of the richest, best preserved and largest of Scotland's prehistoric monuments. The Westness Walk on Rousay is described as being the most important archaeological mile in Scotland.

You can take a car over to all three of these islands if you wish, or you can book a tour of Rousay which collects and delivers you back to the ferry and includes a guide to the main attractions. Rousay is 5¼ miles x 4½ miles/8 x 7km approximately in size and is hilly. The ferry from Tingwall on West Mainland delivers you to Brinian in about 30 minutes with some services returning via Egilsay and Wyre. From Kirkwall, take the A965 to Finstown and turn right on the A966 until you reach the sign (to the right) for the Tingwall Ferry. The population is now c. 227 (1901: 829)

Your tour of the island's circular road should include the Mid Howe Cairn and nearby Mid Howe Broch. The former is so important – the largest known stalled-cairn – that it is protected by a modern building built over it. However start at the Rousay Heritage Centre to get an overview first (it is free). The cairn is a burial chamber and called a stalled-cairn because the bodies were laid in little cells reminiscent of cattle stalls. From the Pier at Brinian, go left on the island's ring road until you reach Eynhallow island, a large flat island between the Mainland and Rousay. Look out for the pull in at a sign for Mid Howe Broch and Cairn. It is about 2miles/3km with great views across Eynhallow Sound. Access is down a path (steepish in places) to the shoreline, about 250ft/80m below. There is what looks like a large barn and on its right is the broch. It is well worth the effort.

Access to the barn is always open and be ready for a surprise. The cairn is huge with a central aisle with stalls where bodies were placed. This is why it is called a stalled cairn.

There were remains of 25 people here. You can climb a gantry and look down into the cairn at either end, or walk the entire length. This cairn was 3,500 years old, dating from the Stone Age when the broch was built, as a fortified tower in the first century AD. It is the largest, but not the longest, stalled cairn in the country.

Just off the road to the Mid Howe cairn and broch are three much smaller stalled cairns, Taversoe Tuick, Blackhammer and Knowe of Yarso. They are always open and admission is free. All are naturally lit inside and signposted on the ring road. The broch is a round, massively built structure which not only served as a home literally within its circular wall, but was strongly fortified to resist attack.

The broch is a structure unique to Scotland and c. 500 are known of which approximately 100 are to be found in Orkney; a similar amount in Shetland. Mid Howe Broch is, sparing just three-four others, without equal. It is incredible that these structures have withstood the passage of time – two or more millenia, let alone depredation by man in that time. The top portion, which was not so massive, had indeed gone, but the main part of it survives relatively intact.

Both the cairn (the building containing it looks like a large barn, with a rounded roof) and the broch are situated on the coast. It is about 2miles/3km with great views across Eynhallow Sound. Continuing over to the other side of the island look out for the old kiln built onto the end of a croft on your right. Upon reaching the coast again, you pass a disused

Mid Howe broch, Rousay. The stalled cairn is just off to the left

Brinian, where the Tingwall ferry docks, Rousay

Opposite top: Egilsay Church ***Bottom:*** St Magnus's monument, Egilsay

mill with a large lake behind it. If you fancy strolling on a small beach with the sound of the sea and seabirds for company, you can gain access close to this old mill. It is at Nousty Sand at the north-east corner of the lake.

There are large colonies of guillemots, kittewakes and fulmars on the western cliffs, but beware some of the cliffs at Scarbra Head and in the north east near Faraclett Head are considered to be dangerous. Just south of Scarbra Head and opposite Eynhallow Island is the Westness Walk. It is about a mile long and takes you past a whole host of prehistoric, Iron Age and Viking sites, together with reminders of the 19th century clearances.

You complete a trip around the island with memorable views over to Egilsay (look for the Viking Church described below), Wyre and other islands including of course the Orkney Mainland.

Egilsay Island

Situated off the east coast of Rousay, it is 3 miiles/5km long and 1 mile/2km wide. The church (St. Magnus Kirk) is a rare example of a Viking round-towered stone church. It is now roofless and stands in a field (free access). It was built between 1116 and 1136AD. It is off the island's spine road with public access. There is a ro-ro ferry from Tingwall, via Rousay and Wyre Island. Both the latter and Egilsay are low-lying, pastoral with some moorland.

Near the church is a memorial to Earl Magnus of Orkney, betrayed by his cousin Haakon and killed on Egilsay in 1116AD. The memorial is believed to be at the site of the treachery. Magnus's remains were found in 1919 behind stonework in the south arcade of the cathedral in Kirkwall.

The skull bore the macabre hole where he had been killed with an axe. The memorial is on the northern edge of the RSPB reserve. The latter has a small colony of corncrakes. Its waters are home to many waders and there is also a wealth of wildflowers in its meadows.

Wyre Island

Off the southwest coast of Rousay is this small island, being 2m/3km by 1m/2km in size. It has a 12th century ruined Viking Castle and chapel. There is a Heritage Centre about island life and its Viking heritage. Ro-ro ferry from Tingwall via Rousay.

Eynhallow Island

A tiny deserted island off the southwest coast of Rousay. There are remains of three prehistoric sites and a 12th century monastery.

Visitor Information

Orkney Ferries from Tingwall on West Mainland. Advance bookings are requested from passengers to Egilsay and Wyre. Although a ro-ro ferry, the number of vehicle places is limited; advance bookings advisable and essential on some services. There is a connecting bus between Kirkwall and Tingwall together with a more limited service from Stromness. The buses leave for Tingwell from the Travel Centre. If you intend calling for a short while on Egilsay or Wyre, you need to plan your times and check the detail through with the ferry company in advance. Otherwise you may be disappointed on finding yourself there for longer than anticipated.
☎ 01856 872004
E: info@orkneyferries.co.uk

Accommodation on Rousay

Hotels / B&B

Taversoe Hotel and B&B
The bar is open to non-residents.
☎ 01856 821325
W: www.taversoehotel.co.uk

Greenfield B&B
☎ 07719 355330/01856 821248

Self Catering

Trumland Farm and hostel
2 self-catering units. Bike hire.
☎ 01856 821252

Faraclett Cottage
☎ 01856 821228

Food

Available at Taversoe Hotel.
☎ 01856 821325
Pier Restaurant and pub (above the ferry landing.)

Places to Visit

Rousay Heritage Centre
☎ 01856 821374/821359
Just off the ferry landing (the pier).
There are toilets and shower here. Un-manned static displays on natural history and archaeology of Rousay.

Trails

There are two trails on the island, the Westness Walk and the Faraclett Head Walk. Taversoe Tuick: Unusual two-storey cairn, near the pier. See text above for the other main archaeological sites. Acess to all free and at all times.
Trumland Gardens: Open: May-Oct, Mon-Fri 10am-5pm.
RSPB Trumland Reserve: above Trumland House. Waymarked trail. For more information contact RSPB Warden on Egilsay Island.
☎ 01856 8221395

Tours

Rousay Tours and Taxis
☎ 01856 821234/07786 169364
E: patrickmaguire@hotmail.co.uk

Stronsay

Of irregular shape caused by the indentation of several bays – Mill Bay, Odin Bay, Bay of Houseby, Bay of Holland and St. Catherine's Bay – it is just over 7m/11km long and is similar in width at its southern end, including the expanse of Bay of Holland. It is low in height, reaching 151 ft/46m at Burgh Hill in the south west. The island is 12 miles/19km north-east of Kirkwall. The population is c. 343 (1901: 1,159).

Off the north-west coast lies the small island of Linga Holm, owned by the Scottish Wildlife Trust. It is a breeding ground for seals and for greylag geese. To the north is Holm of Huip Island, to the north-west lies Papa Stronsay, now a monastery owned by the Transalpine Redemptionists. The islands are breeding grounds for Atlantic grey seals, with large colonies. Like Sanday, there are stunning white-sand beaches and large bays.

Stronsay had a heyday as a herring port, landing up to 12,000 tons in a year. Up to 300 boats used to land at Whitehall Village and many people were employed curing and packing the fish. However a decline set in the 1930s and the fish market is now a visitor centre, café and hostel. At its height, over 5,000 people were employed in the trade. The long row of houses at Whitehall is a reminder of those days, when many more people lived here.

Naturalists will be interested in two

lochs - Meikle Water in the middle of the island and Lea Shun in the south. Both have wildfowl and interesting plant species, especially Lea Shun, where on the adjacent beach can be found the blue flowered Oyster Plant. The Pow (pool) to the east on the Bay of Houseby is home to the white thistle and Patagonia ragwort.

In the east on Odin Bay is the magnificent Vat of Kirbister (a natural arch). The area has some stunning cliff scenery and a nature walk has been made for the convenience of visitors. Opposite, on the west coast is the Hillock of Baywest, an unexcavated stalled-cairn with a broch to the north with an extensive Iron Age village. There are some significant archaeological sites on the island indicating settlement from at least Neolithic times (eg the Ward of Housebay and a Maes Howe type of structure 8ft/2.5m in height). Stronsay, with its large sandy beaches has much to offer and is blessed by not only regular ferry connections but an airport too.

Look out for details of the Stronsay Beast, washed up in 1808. A contemporary drawing shows it with a long neck and tail and six legs. It was 55ft/17m long.

Visitor Information

Orkney Ferries operate a daily service to Stronsay and Eday (except no (summer) service to Eday on on Sunday and only two on Sundays from Kirkwall to Stronsay and one to Kirkwall from Stronsay). Several services require advance booking for vehicles and two of the three boats are restricted to 25 cars maximum; so book ahead!
☎ 01856 872044.

By Air

Loganair fly from Kirkwall to Stronsay Airport.
☎ 01856 872494/873457
No Sunday flights.

Accommodation

Stronsay Hotel
Whitehall Village
☎ 01857 616213
E: stronsayhotel@stronsay.co.uk

B&B

Clestrian: ☎ 01857 616340
Claremont: ☎ 616478
Helmsley: ☎ 616369
Stryme: ☎ 616259
Grindalea: ☎ 616256

Hostel
Stronsay Fish Market, Whitehall Village.
☎ 01857 616386

Stronsay Bird Reserve
Castle, Mill Bay
☎ 01857 616363

Car Hire/Taxi
☎ 01857 616335

Boat Trips
The monks offer a free boat ride to Papa Stronsay. By appointment and weather permitting.
☎ 01857 616389

Shopping
Olivebank
☎ 01857 616255
General stores, butcher and petrol.

Post Office
☎ 01857 616217

Ebenezer Stores
☎ 01857 616339
General store, grocery, frozen food and souvenirs

Above: Whitehall village, Stronsay

Below: Coastline near the Vat of Kirbister, Stronsay

Stronsay Arts and Crafts
Whitehall Village
☎ 01857 616434

Stronsay Craft Shop and Workshop
☎ 07760 373662

Swimming Pool
☎ 01857 616331

Events
Stronsay Gala Day: July

Eday

The island of Eday is 7½m/12km long and 2½m/4km wide. It is 14m/23km NNE of Kirkwall and lies almost half way between Sanday and Egilsay and also between Westray and Stronsay. The outlying islands of Faray and Holm of Faray lie a short distance of the south west corner of Westray. Population c.121 (1901: 596).

Relatively low lying, much of the interior is covered with heather and like its neighbours, Eday has high cliffs, sandy beaches, much evidence of prehistoric occupation and impressive birdlife.

The Eday Ranger can offer guided walks, some at regular times and others on request. There was no great export of herring from here to match nearby Stronsay, but its sandstone was used in the building of Kirkwall Cathedral. It was obtained from a quarry at Ferness on the west coast. Today, it is the birdlife which helps to stimulate tourism and through that, the island's economy, with seabirds such as the puffin, guillemot, cormorant, razorbills, skuas and terns at Mill Loch. Eday has one of the densest populations of red-throated divers in the whole of the British Isles. A bird hide is available there. In the heathland of the south near Flaughton, you may be lucky to spot the whimbrel at its only breeding location in Orkney.

There are various prehistoric settlement sites on the north east island of Calf of Eday. One site is one of the most important in Britain with houses, chambered tombs and field boundaries. There are also important remains of a 17th century salt works. The island is currently uninhabited.

Visitor Information

Orkney Ferries from Kirkwall, daily, pre-booking advisable. A ro-ro ferry taking 25/32 cars depending upon the vessel. This service links with Sanday and Stronsay ☎ 01856 872044.

By Air

Loganair flights to London Airport (named after nearby Bay of London) from Kirkwall, Wednesdays, 2 flights only.
☎ 01856 872494/873457

Accommodation

B&B

Green & The Ruah
Also secluded self-catering cottage
☎ 01857 622263
W: www.redhouseeday.co.uk

Blett
Carrick Bay, Eday KW17 2AB
☎ 01857 622248

Ferness Farms
Eday KW17 2AA
☎ 01857 622262

Groatha
Eday KW17 2AA
☎ 01857 622338

The Roadside Pub/B&B
☎ 01857 622303

Sui Generis B&B
☎ 01857 622219

Self Catering

Swenstay Croft House & Bothy
☎ 01857 622262

Youth Hostel (SYHA affiliated)
☎ 07977 281084

London Airfield, Eday
☎ 01857 622257

Eday Shop
☎ 01857 622283

Post Office
☎ 01857 622339

Guided Walks
Eday Ranger
☎ 07908 148004
A free walking guide to Eday is available from Visitor Centres. It includes six short walks and details of what to see en-route.

Eday Heritage Visitor Centre
☎ 01857 622283
Open: Easter – Mid October, 9am – 6pm; winter – Wed & Sun only, 10am –5pm. Cafe.

Old North School Classroom
☎ 01857 622225
Old school display and submarine display. Entry free. Open most days.

Redhouse Croft
☎ 01857 622217
Ring for opening times
Restoration of c. 19th century croft/watermill Tearoom, plus evening meals (booking essential)

Sui Generis
☎ 01857 622219
Furniture workshop and galleries/gardens; appointment only

Car Hire/Taxi
☎ 01857 622206/07739 286350

Eday Minibus Tours
☎ 01857 622206
Mon, Wed, Fri - May - August, please book ahead. Will fit in with ferry times if on day visit from Kirkwall. Bike hire also available.

Sanday

Situated to the east of Eday Island and some 15 miles/24km north east of Kirkwall, this smaller spindly island is c. 14 miles/22km in length. It is comprised chiefly of sand, is relatively flat (the Wart being the highest point at 213ft/65m. Population c. 550 (1901: 1,727). There are memorable beaches favoured by seals as well as humans. Sanday has large colonies of both Atlantic grey and Common seals. It is easy to reach, being served by ferry from Kirkwall (on a daily basis in summer) and has an airport. The ferry takes 1 hour 25 minutes direct, 20 minutes longer if via Eday.

Of all the small Scottish islands where you are always within a mile of the sea (or thereabouts), Sanday is the largest with two communities at Kettletoft and Lady, separated by the airport. The island is aligned from the south west to the north east with the ferry terminal at the far south west point (at Loth).

Sanday boasts the Quoyness Chambered Tomb, thought to be c. 4,000 years old, near Kettletoft. It has a central chamber and six cells off it. A find in 1991 caused great excitement. It was at Scar near Burness on the north-west coast. Here was a Viking boat burial with three interments accompanied by high quality ornaments, household

Above: German destroyer – The wreck of German WW1 destroyer B98
at Bay of Lopness, Sanday

Below: Whitemill Bay, Sanday

Opposite page top: Beach on the west coast of Eday looking towards Rousay
in the distance **Bottom:** Cottage overlooking Calf Sound, Eday

goods, gaming pieces and a sword. There was also a richly carved plaque made from whalebone with two heads of dragons similar to those carved on the prow of their boats. Shortly after the excavation was concluded, the site was washed away in a storm. However, all the timbers had rotted away completely. Schei and Moberg state that it is perhaps the finest of its kind ever discovered, dating from the mid–10th century.

In the far north east near North Loch is a SSSI at Northwaa. It is a wetland area with waders, ducks, swans and rich plant life. Look out for the several small trails, including one that runs down the east side of Cata Sand, south east of Lady. This tidal area teems with waders and common seals can be seen here.

Visitor Information

Orkney Ferries from Kirkwall, daily in summer, some service via Eday, pre-booking may be advisable and is essential on some services. Vehicle check-in, 20 minutes prior to departure.
☎ 01856 872044

By Air

Loganair, Mon-Sat, only one flight on Saturdays in each direction
☎ 01856 872494/873457

Sanday Package tour

Minimum four persons. Tour of island, pick up from and return to ferry. Includes packed lunch. Mon, Wed, and Fri, May-September.
☎ 01857 600467

Ferry Bus

From Lady Village, ☎ 01857 600467/600284

Accommodation

Kettletoft Hotel
☎ 01857 600217
W: www.kettletofthotel.com

B&B

Ladybank
☎ 01857 600339

Backaskaill
☎ 01857600305

Bowbells
☎ 01857 600281

Marygarth Manse
☎ 01857 600281

Self catering

Anchor Cottage
☎ 01857 600296 (sleeps 6)

Little Lonnie
☎ 01245 356123 (sleeps 4)

Quoyayre
☎ 01857 600348 (sleeps 4/6)

West Silverhall
☎ 01857 600274 (sleeps 4/6)

Park
☎ 01857 600403 (sleeps 3)

Upperhouse
☎ 01857 600383 (sleeps 5)

Hostel

Ayres Rock
☎ 01857 600410
self-catering or B&B/evening meal 4*

Places to Visit

Quoyness Chambered Tomb
Admission free, open daily

Northwaa SSSI
Wetland area in the north east

Sanday Ranger
☎ 01857 600341

Golf Club
See notice on clubhouse, east of Lady village, nine holes.

Shops
Corses Shop, near Cross Kirk; General store, petrol;
Kettletoft Stores; General store, petrol;
Roadside Shop, Lady village; General store, petrol
There is a Post Office in Kettletoft and Lady and craft shops at Upper Breckan and Ayres Rock.

Car & Taxi Hire
Kettletoft Garage
☎ 01857 600321

Marygarth Manse
☎ 01857 600284
Also cycle hire and mini bus tours

Airfield Hut
☎ 01857 600346

Sanday Tourism Association
☎ 01857 600410

Sanday Show: early August

Swimming Pool
☎ 01857 600310

Westray

Separated from Rousay Island by Westray Firth, it is 23 miles/37km north of Kirkwall. The island is 10 miles/16km long and, at its widest, 6 miles/9km. Population c. 600 (1901: 1,956). Raising beef cattle is a mainstay of the island's economy along with tourism and fishing for white fish, crab and lobster. There is a good export market for the Velvet Crab, processed at Pierowall. Tourists come for the stunning scenery, birdlife plus those who feel the need to fly to Papa Westray, the shortest scheduled flight in the world, just to say they have done it. It takes a couple of minutes and the record has been held since c. 1980. Make sure you claim your certificate to prove you have done it!

The quality of the birdlife is reflected in the RSPB Reserve at Noup Head in the north west of the island. Here the cliffs are five miles in length and the northern section houses the reserve. Only St. Kilda exceeds the numbers of breeding seabirds. A survey (admittedly in 1994) found that the cliffs were home to 44,000 guillemots, 12,700 kittiwakes, 1,600 razorbills and 1,100 fulmars. Since that date there has been a sharp rise in the number of gannets breeding here. The puffin is also well represented here and at the Castle o' Burrian just north of the Rapness Ferry Terminal in the south east of the island. Nearby Stranger Head has a varied seabird population worth visiting.

Westray has its own species of vole, is home to the rare purple primrose *primula scotica* (which also grows well on Papa Westray, Rousay etc). Look out too for angelica around Pierowall Bay. It is thought to have been introduced by the Vikings.

The main centre is Pierowall, the northern of the two ferry terminals where services leave for Papa Westray. The village has a good range of services, with two stores and a gift shop, bakery, swimming pool, golf course, cycle hire etc. The Westray Heritage Centre at Pierowall is a 4★ attraction and other attractions include a Faerie Museum and Gallery and the Wheeling Steen Gallery incorporating the deck cabin of a 19th century sailing ship. A pottery and various craft shops complete a comprehensive range of visitors attractions.

There is a west Westray Trail which starts near Letto Sand and follows the coast to Mae Sand before cutting across to the north west to Bay of Kirbest. From here the trail follows the cliffs all the way to Noup Head. This is a good 6 miles/10km from the start, quite a bit of the return being by road which gives the option of cycling, organising a taxi or getting on with the walking. The views are stunning but keep clear of the cliff edge at all times. An alternative and shorter route is to start at Kirbest and return down the same route.

While in the north, don't overlook Noltland Castle, built in the 16th century and intended as a refuge for Mary, Queen of Scots, in the event of her escaping the clutches of the English Queen, Elizabeth I.

Westray has been awarded Fairtrade Island status.

Visitor Information

Orkney Ferries from Kirkwall. The service also links with Papa Westray. Direct it is 1 hour 25 minutes. In summer there are services daily. Pre-booking is advisable, essential on some services. There are occasional inter island connections (excluding scheduled Papa Westray services).
☎ 01856 872044.

By Air

Loganair service from Kirkwall daily. Two flights per day except Saturday and Sunday (only one).
☎ 01856 872494/873457

Ferry Bus ☎ 07789 034289

Car Hire ☎ 01857 677374

Bus Service ☎ 01857 677450
Sunday service needs to be pre-booked

Wildlife guide ☎ 01857 677777

Accommodation
Hotels
Cleaton House Hotel
☎ 01857 677508
W: www.cleatonhouse.co.uk

Pierowall Hotel
☎ 01857 677472
W: www.pierowallhotel.co.uk

B&B
No 1 Broughton
☎ 01857 677726
W: www.no1broughton.co.uk

Self Catering
Bis Geos 3-4* (sleeps 2-8)
☎ 01857 677420
W: www.bisgeos.co.uk

Seaquoys 4*
☎ 01857 871169
E: kjoddie@hotmail.com

There are several more self catering and B&B properties. Contact Westray Tourist Information Centre ☎ 01857 677777.

Hostel & Camping
The Barn, Chalmersquoy 4* hostel
☎ 01857 677214
E: info@thebarnwestray.co.uk

General Stores/Gifts
Post Office, Skelwick (plus petrol); **Rendalls**, Pierowall (plus petrol); **Tulloch**, Pierowall **Hume Sweet Hume**, Pierowall
☎ 01857 677259
Gifts, off licence, soft furnishings and knitwear

Boat Tours
Sea Life Westray
☎ 01857 677214
Trips to Faray Island; cruises etc

Above: Bay of Pierowall, Westray

Below: Cliffs on the west coast of Westray

Tom Rendall, Habour-master
Gill Pier
☎ 01857 677216
Papa Westray as required

Pierowall Charters
6 Gill Pier, KW17 2DL
☎ 01857 677318
E: bookings@pierowallchartes.co.uk

Tourist Information Centre
Haff Yok Café, Pierowall
☎ 01857 677777
W: www.westraypapawestray.com

Westraak Tours
Quarry Rd, Pierowall KW17 2DH
☎ 01857 677 777
Guided tours of Westray all year round

Cycle Hire
☎ 01857 677319/677374/677777

Places to Visit

Westray Heritage Centre
Pierowall
☎ 01857 677414

Orkney Faerie Museum & Gallery
☎ 01857 677320
Admission free

Wheeling Steen Gallery
Nr the airfield
☎ 01857 677292
Open: Mon-Sat, 10-5pm; winter 12noon-5pm
Gallery and tearoom
Inside the gallery is the deck cabin of a 19th
century shipwreck subsequently used as a
house for 123 years

Westray Knitters
Gorn
☎ 01857 677366

Café
Haff Yok Café, Pierowall
☎ 01857 677568

Westray Pottery
☎ 01857 677776

The Gallery
Pierowall
☎ 01857 677770

Swimming Pool
☎ 01857 677430
Walks leaflet free and widely available on the
island

Golf
Westray has a 9-hole links course
☎ 01857 677303

Papa Westray

This island is known as Papay to the
locals. It sits just over 1 mile to the
east of Westray with the world record
shortest scheduled (two minutes) air
flight from its airfield to Westray making
the island well known and with an
additional source of income. There is a
population of c. 70 people. (1901: 295).
It is 3.75m/6km in length and nowhere
is more than ½ mile from the sea. The
ferry boats dock at the new pier at the
southern end of the island. There is a
trail around the whole coastline, a little
of it on the eastside being by road in
the middle section.

Off the north coast, the Atlantic meets
the North Sea and the waters of one
don't mix easily with the other, creating
a tidal race and sometimes a maelstrom
of water. The island has a massive cave
on its north coast, not referred to in
tourist board literature, but the sea there
is perhaps best avoided. The centre of
the community is Beltane in the middle
of the island. Here is the shop, run by
an island co-operative, who also run the
adjacent guest house and Youth Hostel.

The footpath around the coast keeps

you in touch with most of the island's wildlife except for the RSPB Reserve at North Hill. Holm of Papay Island off the east coast has more birdlife as well as a prehistoric chambered cairn or burial site, rated as one of the best in Orkney.

The plant life is prolific, especially on the mochair grassland growing on blown sand. There is also a good colony of the rare *primula scotica* growing on the north east coast of Fowl Craig. Look for their purple flowers in mid summer.

The heritage of the island includes three impressive sites. The Knap of Howar on the west coast (near the airport) is the earliest existing house in northern Europe and is c. 5,500 years old. Nearby is Holland Farm with a museum of island farming life. The house was the home of the Traill family, lairds of the island for three centuries. Just to the north of the Knap of Howar and close to the coast is St. Boniface Kirk, a simple stone-built church dating from the 12th century. It is one of the oldest Christian sites in the north of Scotland. Not far from the Kirk and exposed on the shore beneath it is Munkerhoose, a settlement occupied between Bronze Age and medieval times. If you found Maeshowe of interest on Orkney Mainland the island has the largest tomb of this kind. It has a long chamber with a dozen cells off it and is known as 'The Disses of the Holm'.

The island has been awarded Freetrade Island status.

Visitor Information

Orkney Ferry from Kirkwall via Westray. Prior booking for some services essential. If you are going direct to Papa Westray from Pierowall

on Westray, the passenger only service is free if you are making a direct connection with the ro-ro ferry at Rapness on Westray. Services daily. There is also a Friday vehicle service from Westray which may be subject to cargo operations and also a Kirkwall, North Ronaldsay, Papa, Westray, Kirkwall service on a Tuesday. On a few separate dates the service goes to Papa Westray prior to North Ronaldsay. All these services are weather, and often cargo, permitting, with confirmation the day before sailing.

☎ 01857 677216 for Papa Westray/Westray services.

☎ 01856 872044 for the North Ronaldsay connection service.

By Air

Loganair from Kirkwall, daily. Only 1 flight on Sundays. There are special low cost fares.

Accommodation

B&B

Beltane Guest House
☎ 01857 644224
E: beltanepapay@aol.co.uk
Run by the community Co-op, who also run the Youth Hostel which has two en-suite rooms sleeping 6/7.

School Place
☎ 01857 644268

Self Catering

Holm View, sleeps 4
☎ 07723 367443
E: tomhughes@scotnet.co.uk

Peatwell, sleeps 2-4
E: john.nove@verizon.net

Shopping etc

Co-op Shop
general store, crafts etc. Closed Sundays, staggered opening times.
☎ 01857 644321

Above: Pierowall harbour, Westray

Below: Pierowall village, Westray

Left: Coast near Fowl Craig, Papa Westray   **Right:** The doorway of Knap of Howar at sunset, Papa Westray   **Below:** Knap of Howar, Papa Westray

WFM Brown (bakers)
Gill Pier
☎ 01857 677349

Daybreak Craftshop
☎ 01857 644275

Bewan Gallery & Workshop
☎ 01857 644245

Post Office
Daybreak ☎ 01857 644275

Papey Peedie Island Tours
Full or half day tours. Full tours include lunch
and afternoon tea/coffee break.
☎ 01857 644321

RSPB Warden
North Hill Nature Reserve, guided walks
☎ 01857 644240

Car Hire ☎ 01857 644245

Airport ☎ 01857 644252

Nouster Pier (for yacht facilities)
☎ 01857 644282

Westray/Papa Westray Tourist Association
☎ 01857 677777

Light snacks available at Beltane Guest House
and School Place.

Papey Warden: ☎ 01857 64424

Bothy Museum, at Holland Farm.

**Recycled by Design Workshop & Gallery, by
RSPB reserve.**
☎ 01857644245

North Ronaldsay

The most northerly of Orkney's
Northern Isles. It is 3m/5km long and
2m/3.2km wide, being low and flat with
fertile, sandy soils. Population c. 70 (1901:
442). At times the waters between here
and Sanday Island can be difficult for
shipping. Both Linkelet Bay and Nouster
Bay have attractive beaches of white sand.
Isolation creates its own atmosphere here
despite regular scheduled ferries and
flights plus some concessionary prices
on services. Perhaps it is the better for
it. Uniquely, the sheep are confined by
a wall or dyke to the foreshore to keep
them off agricultural land. They have
developed an appetite for seaweed which
gives the meat a distinctive flavour. As a
result the meat is much sought after. The
dyke is continuous around the island
but ewes in lamb are brought into the
fields in spring.

Like neighbouring islands, the island's
wildlife is an important draw. It is an
important resting place for migratory
birds and there is an annual crop of rare
visitors, perhaps blown of course, each
year. Both common and Atlantic grey
seals frequent the shoreline.

Hugging the shoreline in the north
east of the island, in fact at it most eastern
extremity at Kirk Taing, is the Old
Beacon Lighhouse which was first lit in
1789. In need of restoration, it sprung
to prominence when it reached 3rd
place in the BBC's Restoration Village
programme. It was replaced by the
current lighthouse in 1854 and this 'new'
one is the tallest land-based lighthouse
in the British Isles, at 109 ft.

Another 18th century building is
Holland House in Hollandstown, near
to the airfield. It was built by the Traill
family and their descendants still live
there. The Traills bought the island
in 1729. The gardens have the largest
volume of trees and shrubs on the island.

Of more modern date in the south
west of the island and close to the pier

is the Bird Observatory. Built in 1987, it also offers accommodation and its bar, café and restaurant are open to non-residents.

Visitor Information

Orkney Ferries from Kirkwall, direct and with additional services from Papa Westway. The time from Kirkwall is 2 hours 40 minutes, but note that sailing times are approximate and depend on cargo operations (plus weather). Friday sailings and an additional boat on Tuesday. Occasional Sunday sailings.
☎ 01856 870244

By Air

Loganair from Kirkwall, daily in summer.

Accommodation

Guest House

Bird Observatory (near the pier)
Twingness, KW17 2BE
☎ 01857 633200
En-suite rooms, family rooms and dormitories at the Bird Observatory

Garso Guest House
☎ 01857 633244

Self Catering

Brigg Self Catering
☎ 01857 633244

Dennishill ☎ 01856 874486

Howar Cottage & Nouster Croft, at Howar Conservation Farm
☎ 01857 633253

The Dolls House, Roadside (self catering and B&B)
☎ 01857 633221

Quoybanks (self catering and B&B, evening meal available)
☎ 01857 633221

Shopping

Airfield Goods & Services, general stores and woollen goods. ☎ 01857 633220

Petrol - Hooking ☎ 01857 633257

Taxi, car hire, minibus ☎ 01857 633244

Burrian Inn ☎ 01857 633221

Off Licence/Tea Room/Gifts
☎ 01857 633221

Local Knitwear, Mrs. Donnelly,
☎ 01857 633242

Bank - only open monthly, enquire at Post Office ☎ 01857 633221

A Yarn From North Ronaldsay
Sangar, KW17 2BG
☎ 01857 633297
Processes wool and knitwear from local sheep.

Tours

North Ronaldsay Trust Ltd
W.T. Muir
☎ 01857 633257

Lighthouse & Yarn Company Tours
T & C Muir ☎ 01857 633244

Golf Course - nine holes - ☎ 01857 633242

Lighthouse Visitor Centre
☎ 01857 633297
Cafe, gift shop & bike hire

Left: North Ronaldsay sheep

Below: The Old Beacon at Kirk Taing, North Ronaldsay